"This book belongs to

_____.
It's your special book, just for you!
Write your name nice and big,
So everyone knows it's true!"

Emma loved her sister Mandy more than anything. Mandy was older, taller, and, Emma thought, smarter too. Mandy's bedroom shelves sparkled with shiny trophies and medals from school.

Emma's shelves, however, were filled with sheet music, her well-loved piano books, and a football medal she'd won years ago.

At school, Mandy always seemed to have the answers. She aced spelling tests, wrote stories that teachers read aloud to the class, and always came home with certificates.

Emma, on the other hand, found reading hard. Letters danced on the page, and spelling tests made her stomach flip.

"Why can't I be more like Mandy?" Emma thought.

"Emma, come here!" her mum called one evening. "Look at Mandy's latest certificate. She got top marks in her maths test!"

Emma clapped politely but felt a lump form in her throat.

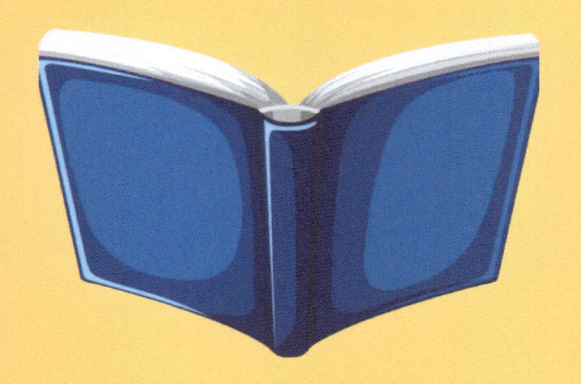

At school, things weren't much better. One day, her teacher asked her to read aloud.

As Emma stumbled over the words, she heard someone whisper, "She's so slow." Her cheeks burned, and she wished she could disappear.

She's so slow!

At dinner that night, Mandy talked about her big science project. Emma sat quietly, poking at her peas.

"Emma," Dad said, "how was your day?"

"It was fine," Emma mumbled, but inside, she didn't feel fine at all.

The next morning, Emma's teacher announced a talent show. "We're looking for singers, performers, and musicians to take part!" he said.

Emma's ears perked up. She loved playing the piano and singing.

At home, Emma practiced her favourite song. Her fingers glided across the piano keys as she sang softly.

"That's beautiful," her mum said.

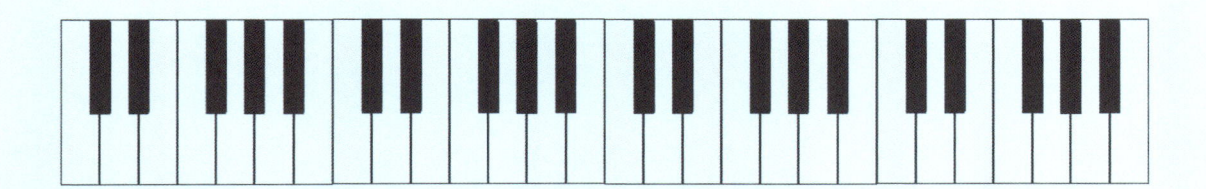

But as the talent show drew closer, doubt crept in.

"What if I make a mistake?" Emma thought. "Mandy would do better."

She decided not to sign up.

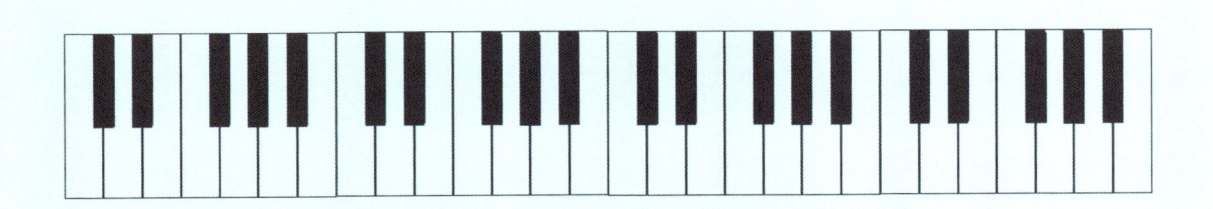

The next day, Emma's teacher noticed she hadn't joined the list.

"Emma, I've heard you sing and play the piano. You have a gift!" the teacher said. "Please think about entering."

Emma hesitated, but she nodded.

That night, Mandy knocked on Emma's door.

"Can I hear you play?" Mandy asked.

"I can't play well, and I'm not a strong singer," Emma said, staring at the floor.

"Let me be the judge of that," Mandy replied with a smile.

When Mandy heard Emma sing and play, her eyes lit up.

"You're amazing, Emma!" she said. "You HAVE to sign up!"

"You really think so?" Emma asked.

"I know so," Mandy said.

With Mandy's encouragement, Emma signed up for the talent show.

The week crawled by as everyone waited for the big day. Emma felt nervous and excited all at once.

Finally, the talent show arrived. As Emma stepped on stage, she took a deep breath and began to play.

Her voice filled the room, and when she finished, the crowd erupted in applause.

"You were brilliant!" Mandy said after the show.

Emma grinned. For the first time, she felt proud of her.

From then on, Emma stopped comparing herself to Mandy. Instead, she focused on her music.

She joined a choir, played in school concerts, and even wrote her own songs.

One day, Emma's teacher gave her a special book written in a dyslexia-friendly font.

"This might make reading easier," the teacher said.

And it did.

Emma still found reading and writing tricky, but now she knew it was okay to learn differently.

"Your mind is like a melody," Mandy said one day. "Unique and beautiful."

Emma's performance in the talent show stayed in her memory for years. Every time she played the piano, she felt a little spark of pride.

It reminded her that everyone has their own way to shine.

At home, Mandy added a new shelf in Emma's room.

"What's this for?" Emma asked.

"For all your awards," Mandy said with a wink.

Emma laughed. "I don't need awards. I have my music."

"And your family," Mandy added. "Don't forget that."

Emma hugged Mandy tightly.

In their beautiful blend of talents and personalities, Emma and Mandy knew one thing for sure: they were better together.

The End

Printed in Great Britain
by Amazon